To my family, friends, Coach Bob, the NBAC, and all of my wonderful fans.
—M. P.

Dream, Plan, Reach
MICHAEL PHELPS
FOUNDATION

To Kayla, Bobby, and Rachel.
—A. A.

To Andrea—my strength.
To Ava and Ezra—my inspiration.
—W. J.

SIMON & SCHUSTER BOOKS FOR YOUNG READERS
An imprint of Simon & Schuster Children's Publishing Division
1230 Avenue of the Americas, New York, New York 10020
Text copyright © 2009 by Michael Phelps
Illustrations copyright © 2009 by Ward Jenkins
All rights reserved, including the right of reproduction in whole or in part in any form.
SIMON & SCHUSTER BOOKS FOR YOUNG READERS is a trademark of Simon & Schuster, Inc.
Book design by Lucy Ruth Cummins
The text for this book is set in Slappy.
The illustrations for this book are rendered digitally.
Manufactured in the United States of America
10 9 8 7 6 5 4 3 2 1
Library of Congress Cataloging-in-Publication Data
Phelps, Michael, 1985–
How to train with a T. rex and win 8 gold medals / Michael Phelps
with Alan Abrahamson ; Illustrated by Ward Jenkins.
p. cm.
ISBN: 978-1-4169-8669-0 (hardcover)
1. Phelps, Michael, 1985-—Juvenile literature. 2. Swimmers—United States Biography—
Juvenile literature. 3. Olympics—Juvenile literature. I. Abrahamson, Alan. II. Title.
GV838.P54P46 2009
797.2'1092—dc22
[B]
2009000379

first
edition

HOW to TRAIN with a T. REX and WIN 8 GOLD MEDALS

MICHAEL PHELPS

with Alan Abrahamson

Illustrated by Ward Jenkins

Simon & Schuster Books for Young Readers

New York London Toronto Sydney

In the summer of 2008, in Beijing, I did something that nobody had ever done. I won eight gold medals!

It took a lot of hard work. How did I do it?

For six years, from 1998 to 2003, I barely took a day off.

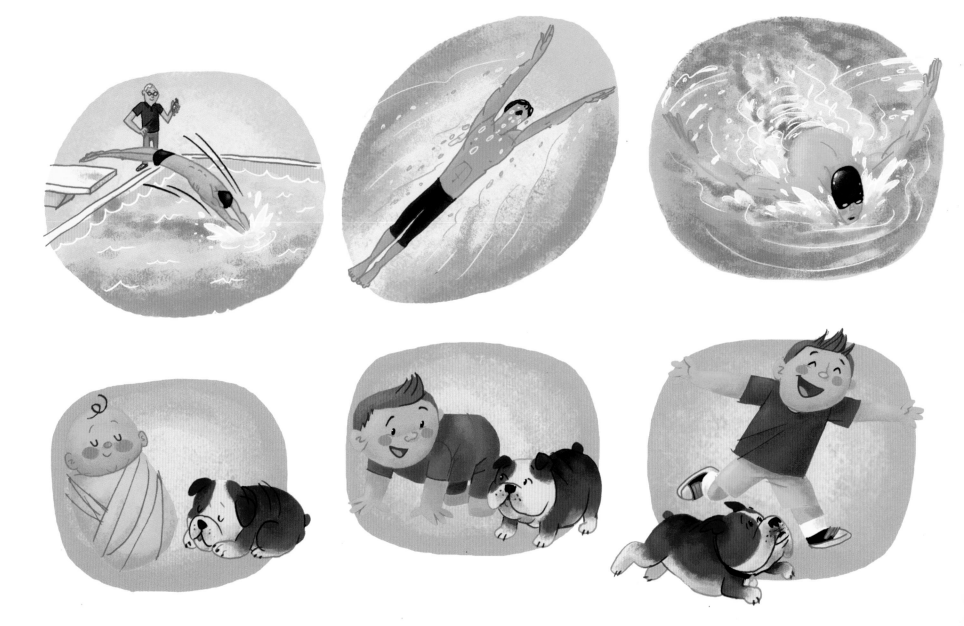

I trained for **six** years!

That's a kindergartener's whole life!

That's the same as **42** dog years!

That's **183,040** trips around the bases!

That's the same as swimming from my hometown of Baltimore to the North Pole and back— and doing it all over again!

PERFECT! NOW DO IT TWO MORE TIMES.

TWO???

That's like swimming the full length of the Great Wall of China **three** times!

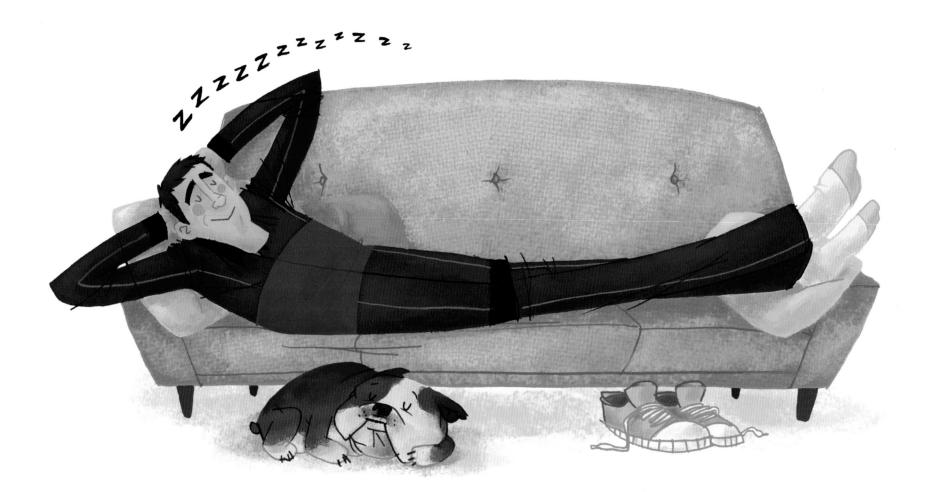

Every day I took a three-hour nap.
That's **6,552** hours of naptime over six years.

Put all together, I napped for **273** days—and
that doesn't even count the sleeping I did at night
during regular bedtime.

273 days?
That's how long it takes
for a baby to grow before it
is born!

That's an NBA
championship team's
entire season!

That's like napping away **three** summer vacations in a row!

To have the energy for so much swimming, I had to eat a lot—as much as **10,000** calories every day.

That's like eating **912** pizzas a year. I could *never* eat that much pizza!

HERMAN

Nearly **half a ton** of pizza!

Half a ton is the same as a small elephant.

Or half a small car.

Or enough broccoli to fill the back of a pickup truck.

I got so strong from training that my legs could press **300** pounds **60** times in one workout. That's **18,000** pounds total, or **nine** tons!

I could leg-press a Tyrannosaurus Rex and **10** velociraptors!

Nine tons is like **55** superstar basketball centers.

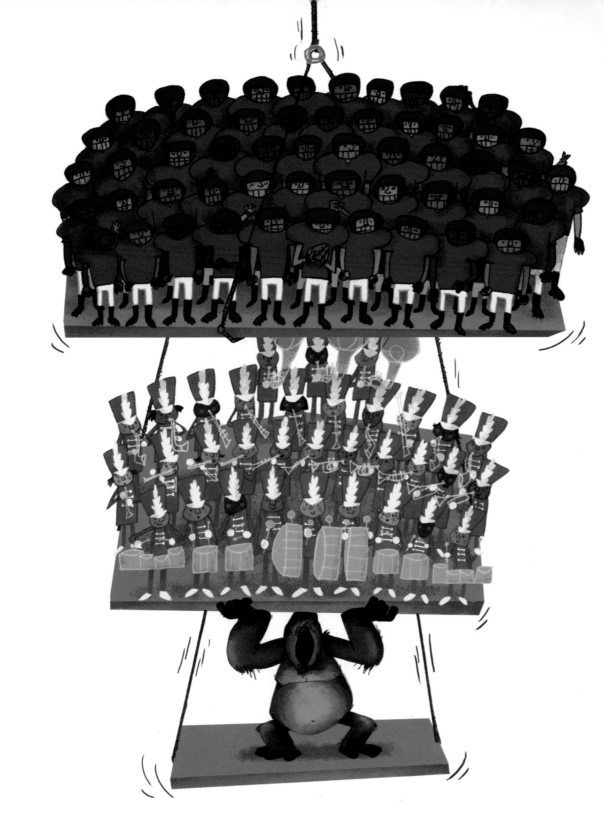

That's the entire **53**-man roster of my favorite football team **and** every single member of a **30**-piece pep band (plus their instruments) **and** an **800**-pound gorilla!

AUGUST

Just to get to the finals, I had to swim **17** races in **nine** days, including **eight** finals. That was a lot of racing—**3,400** meters in the pool.

I SWAM THIS MUCH
19
11
In Beijing alone, I swam more than the length of
19
Washington Monuments laid end to end!

Or the height
of nearly

11

Eiffel Towers
stacked one
on top of
the other!

After **Six** years of training—

swimming more than **60,000** meters in practice each week,

snoozing through **6,552** hours of naps,

eating almost **10,000** calories a day,

leg-pressing **18,000** pounds in a session,

and swimming **3,400** meters in the Olympics—

I won my last individual race, the 100-meter butterfly, by one one-hundredth of a second!

WOW.

One one-hundredth of a second—that's faster than the blink of an eye!

I won by about the
length of a fingernail.
It doesn't get any closer.

I did it! I was the first person to win **eight** gold medals at a single Olympics.

Now I'm setting new goals, and with a lot of hard work, who knows what dreams I will achieve in the future!